George Curtisius

Project Islam 3.0

for

21. Century!

Peace inside Islam and with other Religions

George Curtisius

Self-Publisher: George Curtisius

Contact: **george.curtisius@web.de**

ISBN-13: 978-1511411578

ISBN-10: 1511411570

Dedication

I dedicate this booklet to all Muslims who live in peace with their neighbors and who live in peace with believers of other religions.

I dedicate this booklet to all Islamic teachers and preachers, who teach an Islam, which is free of violence towards other Islamic sects, other religions and religious denominations.

I dedicate this booklet to all Islamic legal scholars, Islamic theologians, imams and muftis who interpret the Koran that other religions are equivalent to Islam and who interpret the Koran in that way that Muslims have to respect in modern societies the constitution of their state they live in.

I also dedicate my booklet to all politicians who respect the Muslims in their country and who struggle that the Islam in their country fits to the life in a modern society of the twenty-first century without violating moral and ethical teachings of Islam.

I dedicate my booklet to all Islamic legal scholars, Islamic theologians, grand imams and grand muftis who are willing to revise the Koran in that way that all guidelines for the life of Muslims can only be understood to live peacefully with other people. There shall be no possibility that Islamist groups can justify their cruel and inhumane actions with reference to the Koran.

Insofar I wish that all Islamic and Non-Islamic Governments support this project for an Islam 3.0.

I thank my dear wife for her suggestions for the title also to single topics and for the examination of the manuscript.

Table of Contents

Preface

Perhaps I am not entitled to give recommendations to renew or revise the Islam. I am not a Muslim. I do not belong to any religious denomination. But I believe in God. And I struggle to serve God. I try to work for peace of nations, of ethnic and religious groups of people. And I feel that there has to be peace between religions and their religious denominations. Because God wants peace!

I am not bound to look at the Islam in a way as Muslims want their Islam to be perceived as a peaceful religion. I perceive the Islam in my country Germany with its positive and negative manifestations. But there is also the image of Islam in other countries. I view on television and read in papers that worldwide in the last years many thousands of people were killed in the name of Islam.

In giving recommendations for peace between religions and religious denominations it might be my advantage that I am not bound to a specific religious denomination. I can look at problems of religions from a higher point of view where it is easier to find the solution for existing problems. At least I can look at the manifestations of Islam from another perspective than a Muslim.

I ask readers for understanding that I am not familiar with the contents of Islamic belief. I only look at the relations and manifestations of Islam to human beings and especially with reference to other religions and other branches of Islam. I feel that the Islam should get a better image than it has hitherto.

Frankly and honestly I really do not know why I name a modern Islam as Islam 3.0. I even do not know what it is when people are speaking of WEB 2.0. But it sounds good a new thing to rename with a digit. 3.0 seems to be more modern that 2.0. That seems to be my intention to name a modernized Islam as Islam 3.0. Why shouldn't we accept this as a chance?

When I feel that Islam should be revised or renewed I mean this in a respectful way. In this project there should be made clear which instructions in the Koran are only historically like the Old Testament in Christian belief and which are valid in today life like the New Testament in Christian belief. It should be achieved that the guidelines of the Koran cannot be any longer misunderstood or misinterpreted to allow the killing of other people might it be Muslims or believers of other religions and their denominations.

I write this booklet under a pseudonym. The reason for this is that I don't want to discuss my views with critics. I am too old to fight heavily for my conviction.

Who doesn't like my views may be looking for readers of my treatise, which share my views as discussion opponents. Under these readers certainly could be found followers of my theses that are ready to discuss them publicly.

With this booklet I would like to sensitize the readers, the responsible heads of governments, politicians and particularly the religious leaders to do more for peace between religions and their religious denominations.

Usually a political book begins with explanations why it is necessary to write this book or why changes are necessary in policy. To make it easier for readers to find out if they should read this book I start with my proposition how Islam 3.0 could be achieved. I explain what has to be done to make the essential changes in comparison with the existing Islam, to make Muslims and their critics more peaceful.

UN Resolution for a Fight against Islamic Terrorism

The Secretary-General of the United Nations and the World Security Council together should call for a special session of the United Nations General Assembly to be held in New York. It could be a General Assembly or only an Assembly of Islamic states, e.g. of Indonesia, Pakistan, Malaysia, Afghanistan, Saudi Arabia, Egypt, Jordan, Iraq, Iran, Lebanon, Syria, Yemen, Algeria, Morocco, Tunisia, Sudan, Nigeria etc.

In this General Assembly the Heads of Governments or States of all Islamic countries should be asked to make their contribution to stop Islamist terrorism.

Governments cannot defeat terrorism with weapons and with violence if it is based on religious motives like an ideology. Also a clampdown on jihadists with seizure and punishment won't help. This battle cannot be won on the level of physical actions.

To stop Islamist terrorism the underlying religious motives have to be refuted. Religious motives like an ideology are a spiritual power. With weapons one can kill people but cannot kill spiritual motives.

All Islamic states, which want a peaceful Islam can contribute to stop Islamist terrorism in the following way.

With the agreement of the Heads of Government of Islamic states the Secretary-General invites to an international conference. In this conference meet in conclave like a secluded retreat all leading Islamic theologians, it means all Islamic legal scholars, grand imams, and grand muftis of all Islamic states.

It is well known that selected cardinals of the Roman Catholic Church who meet in conclave in the Vatican Palace elect the Roman Catholic Pope. The cardinals are only allowed to leave the conclave if the new pope is elected. The cardinals are secluded from the outside world.

Also industrial companies use retreats, sealed from the outside world, until a special problem is solved.

In Islam also the method of a secluded retreat should be used. I call now this secluded retreat a convention.

The place of this Islam convention could be Mecca in Saudi Arabia or Cairo in Egypt or Geneva in Switzerland.

During this convention the invited Islamic theologians, Islamic legal scholars, grand imams and grand muftis or elected representatives of Islamic states where no Islamic spiritual head exists confer with each other what they recommend as Islam 3.0, a revised and unified form of Koran for the modern world. The purpose is that the Koran is in a spiritual way revised to make sure that the Koran can no longer be misinterpreted to justify violence or disparagement against other Muslims or believers of other religions.

The Roman Catholic Church, and the Christian Orthodox Churches have a spiritual head called pope or patriarch. Even all Protestant Churches have a head of their denomination or at least a speaker, representing their organization in public.

Unlike the Roman Catholic Church or Christian Orthodox Churches in Islam there exists no spiritual head for the whole Islamic world. Even in most Islamic countries there seems to be no spiritual head representing all theologians, imams, muftis and being responsible for them.

Instead of repeating the whole spiritual line of Islamic theologians, Islamic legal scholars, imams and muftis I use henceforth only the names "imams and muftis".

It seems therefore necessary that in each of all Islamic countries their imams or muftis elect a representative who shall participate in the convention for Islam 3.0. The elected representative should submit his voters his ideas where he wants to see amendments or changes to avoid possible false interpretations of the Koran. Together with his colleagues who elected him as a representative of their country a concept is worked out that the representative takes to the conventions as the contribution of his country for Islam 3.0.

The governments of all Islamic states are requested to arrange for that in their Islamic state a spiritual head is elected and that a concept for improvements of the Koran can be brought into the discussions of the international convention for Islam 3.0.

I recommend that also the Muslim associations in Germany, France, U.K. and Italy are invited to send each of them an imam as representative of their Muslim population to the convention.

This convention for Koran revision for Islam 3.0 will only end when all participants have achieved a result they have agreed to.

After having finished a satisfactorily revision of the Koran for Islam 3.0 a worldwide conference should take place. To this conference all leading Islamic theologians respectively imams and muftis out of countries are invited, which had not sent a representative to the convention. In this conference the authors of the revised Koran present the results of their collective work. They substantiate their work and ask for approval. With the approval of 95 percent of all Islamic theologians present the revised Koran for

Islam 3.0 consisting out of the new defined parts will be declared as law of Islam.

Misinterpretations of the Koran and deviations other as described in the Koran are forbidden. No Muslim is authorized to interpret in the Koran what he likes.

As a next step in each Islamic state and in countries with a significant number of Muslims the revised Koran for Islam 3.0 is presented to local imams.

An Islam 3.0 has as result uniform guidelines for the life of Muslims. It allows worldwide a uniform training of imams.

Islam Convention for Islam 3.0

The spiritual heads of the large Islamic states meet in a convention secluded from the outside world. In this convention they bring their ideas and proposals to renew or adapt the Koran for the modern civilization.

I repeat. The purpose should be that the Koran is in a spiritual way revised to make sure that the Koran can no longer be misinterpreted to justify violence or disparagement against other Muslims or believers of other religions.

It has to be achieved that the Koran does not be any longer a basis of uncertainty or doubts in relation to the interpretation of its contents.

The problem is that the Koran in its existing form allows various possibilities for misinterpretation or even abusive misinterpretation. It should be the task of the convention to eliminate such problems. The convention should not end before the assembly has worked out unanimously the necessary changes of the Koran.

Removal of Causes of Islamist Terrorism

I have several reasons to write this booklet. One reason is that people in my home country Germany experience the threat posed by radicalized Muslims or so-called Islamists. The society I live in is no longer free from Islamist terrorism and the danger of terrorism. It guarantees no longer the security on which we could trust in former years.

The second reason is that the Islamic State (IS) in Iraq and Syria has committed barbarous deeds. The head or proclaimed Caliph of this state IS is Abu Bakr al-Bagdhadi, who has obtained a BA, MA and PhD in Islamic studies. The IS has justified its cruel crimes with teachings in the Koran. The Non-Islamic world had to believe that Caliph Dr. al-Baghdadi as an expert in Islamic theology knows what is right. It was profoundly irritating for the Non-Islamic world that the teachings of the Koran would allow barbarous murders.

Since years is known that under the name of Islam there have been committed terroristic attacks with bombs and gunfire, even with suicide attacks, from Sunnis against Shiites, and vice versa, also from Sunnis against infidels in countries like Pakistan, Afghanistan, Iraq, Syria, Libya, Nigeria, Somalia, Kenya, Yemen and others. I think that such crimes have to be terminated.

The third reason is that Queen Rana of Jordan demanded some time ago in her speech on a conference in Dubai that the Islamic theologians should explain unmistakably what the Islam stands for.

Recently Abd al-Fattah as-Sisi, President of Egypt, gave a

speech at the university Al-Azhar in Cairo. It has been reported of him to have said the following: "The ummah of 1.6 billions faithful Muslims has not to become a source of fear, danger and destruction." He continued: The Islamic community tears itself, it is on the road to perdition." He also said: You "bear the responsibility before God. The world expects your word. We need a contemporary discourse". I have found these words of as-Sisi in the article of Josef Joffe "Islamistischer Terror - Fluch der Ideologie" in ZEIT ONLINE, 15.01.2015, and translated them into English.

The German chancellor, too, requested that the Muslim associations should clear what the Islam really is.

I have read a number of articles about the Islam in German online papers written by Islamic scientists. These articles helped me to submit my proposal to the world of Islam.

The Proposed New Layout of the Koran

Part 1

Part one contains suras, which are obligatory and helpful for the life of Muslims. These are the guidelines for pious Muslims. It should contain only guidelines for a peaceful life to give evidence that the Islam is peaceful religion. Part 1 should be complemented by guidelines for the modern world, which the original Koran could not foresee.

Helpful would be an annex to part 1, which contains obligatory and unmistakable interpretations of the suras and guidelines.

Part 2

Part two should contain everything of the Koran, which is only part of history or referring to the history of Islam and which makes the Islam appear as a religion of violence.

In his article in Süddeutsche Zeitung, 20.01.2015, "Religion und Gewalt – Der Islam braucht eine kritikfähige Renaissance" the Islam scientist Abdel-Hakim Ourghi from the German College of Education in Freiburg named some examples for the historical Koran, which refer to violence in Islam.

He described that the Clan Banu Qaynuqa' as opponents of Muhammad had to leave Medina without their belongings (Koran 3, 12-13). The same happened to the tribe of Banu an-Nadir (Koran 59, 2-3). The background of sura 33, verses 26-27 is the mass execution in April 627 of 600 men of the third tribe, the Banu Qurayza, also the sale of their women and children as slaves.

This part 2 could therefore contain all parts in the Koran, which refer to combat instead of peace, to retaliation instead of forgiveness and tolerance.

I think it would be helpful to structure the Koran in generally two main components as explained above. To this could be added a third part with recommendations.

Part 1 should contain the guidelines for a devout Muslim. This part contains all original suras, which cannot be misunderstood and which promote peace. It contains guidelines how a Muslim shall live together with other Muslims, in his marriage, with the education of his children etc. It describes also how he shall behave towards Non-Muslims, i.e. the believers of other religions. These guidelines have to be defined in detail in the Koran and made obligatory for all Muslims.

The convention has also to define if equal rights for men and women are part of a modern Islam.

The modernized Koran could contain a core doctrine being worldwide obligatory for all Muslims. For teachings beyond the worldwide common core doctrine modifications may be allowed. Due to culture and history of single countries small deviations could be possible to a more fundamental Islam in Saudi Arabia or to an easier Islam in Europe. The participants of the convention would describe these possible deviations.

Additionally the Islamic legal scholars as participants of the convention should define, which branches in Islam, e.g. Sunnites and Shiites, have to be accepted as core elements of Islam. Furthermore also secondary directions of Islam, e.g. Alawites, Alevites, Sufis and similar sects and their followers should be tolerated as a part of the community of Islam. Against them no violence should be permitted. With the recommended definitions as aforesaid explained religious wars in the name of Islam will be terminated forever.

In an annex to part 1 could be laid down interpretations to part 1, the suras and the other guidelines so that all readers of the Koran can understand unmistakably what is really meant. These interpretations shall help to prevent misinterpretations of the Koran. This would also be of help for the sermons of imams.

It should no longer be possible that radicalized Islamist groups can justify their killings of people, their abductions and raping of women and the sale of women as slaves who are believers of a Non-Islamic religion with reference to the Koran.

Part 2 should contain the history of Islamic belief. That means it has to contain all texts, which can only be understood in their ancient context and which are only meant for the Muslims of that century.

A model for the new layout of the Koran could be the Christian Bible, which is mainly structured in the Old Testament and the New Testament.

The Old Testament is a collection of legends describing the history of the tribes of Israel. The Old Testament describes partially cruel deeds. Among many other legends it is claimed that God Jehova shall have instructed his believers to capture the town Jericho and to kill all inhabitants, even women and children.

Compared with the teachings in the New Testament, in which God is described, as a God of love and mercy, this part of the history in the Old Testament about Jericho is not credible, not plausible. God does not change his mind. God is eternally the same. He is not in former centuries a God of wrath and violence and later a God of love and mercy. Therefore the Old Testament is not a guideline for Christian believers particularly with regard to the fact that it describes the history of the Israelites. Of the Old Testament only the 10 Commandments of Moses serve also Christian believers as a guideline.

For a true Christian is valid the word of Jesus, the Prince of Peace: "Those that live by the sword shall die by the sword". The New Testament is the instruction for life with the main statement of love of neighbors and enemies. It stands for unrestricted peace.

It should be strictly forbidden all Muslims to refer to historical events of violation and surah's linked with them as a guideline for their behavior and related actions.

The third part could contain recommendations for Muslims how they can engage in secular countries where they build the minority to be a good neighbor for people with other religions. This could also include how they become a valuable citizen for their government and for the mayor of the village or town they live in.

With the above procedure there is no harm done to the Koran or the Islam. The revised Koran has not less text passages but rather more text than before. In a metaphorical sense all text passages, which should be practiced by a devout Muslim and which secure a peaceful life are put in a drawer with the label "part 1". All text passages of the actual Koran, which deal with violence against people, are put in a drawer with the label "part 2".

Islam, Islamic Sects and other Religions

What does it mean for a religion and their believers to keep peace with other religions and their believers? First of all it does mean to respect other religions and their believers and to accept them of equal value.

In the past it seemed to me that Muslims were convinced and proclaimed that the Islam is a religion superior to all other religions. They denied that other religions were of equal value. If such a conception is continued and maintained peace between religions cannot be achieved.

If there really exists such a claim of Islam it would contravene with the Jewish belief that Jews are God's chosen people. There is no evidence for any of such claims. God is just. He privileges neither any religion nor any person.

The God of the Christians says that all his human beings are of equal worth and that all of them have a unique and inviolable human dignity. If there are Islam scholars who insist upon that the Islam is superior to other religions and that Muslims are superior to believers of other religions than they are asked whether their God Allah is different to the God of other religions. Could it be that God Allah is more powerful than the God of Christians or other religions? There might be a difference insofar that the Christian God is a God of love and mercy. The Islamic God Allah is a God of mercy, so I read recently. But is this really a difference? Is mercy without love conceivable?

It has been said that the main differences between Sunnis and Shiites have to do with the intensity of religiousness. Sunnis claim to be more religious than the Shiites. If it is commonly accepted that God is a God of love and mercy and of freedom he does not compel or oblige his human beings to maintain a certain degree of religiousness.

God would have had permitted only one religion and no other one as well as no sects if there would be only one way to serve him and to worship him. Why do the Sunnis not accept that there are many different possibilities to worship God and to serve him?

God has not demanded that his human beings on earth have to belong to any religion. He wants that his human beings live a God-filled life and keep his commandments and his laws. A religion can be helpful to lead a God-filled life but is not a prerequisite.

God has neither ordered nor authorized Sunnis to judge or criticize the religiousness of Shiites or believers of other religions. It is only up to Allah to hold his human beings accountable for their actions on the Day of Judgment.

What are the reasons that Sunnis kill Shiites and other believers of Islamic sects and believers of other religions? Sunnis who kill or degrade believers of other sects or religions what have they to expect on the Day of Judgment when Allah judges their ungodly deeds? Isn't it a fact that Sunnites murdering and bombing Shiites in Iraq and Pakistan discredit the Islam? They let appear the Islam as a violent religion and as a source of terrorism. Do the Sunnis like it that their religion is judged as violent and as a source of terrorism?

Because the Sunnis kill Shiites the Shiites revenge and kill Sunnis. This goes on and on. Why Islamic legal scholars of Sunnis don't stop this violence, which is of spiritual damage to the aggressor? The murderers will have to suffer unimaginable times in the hell? Why were the aggressors not warned by their imams not to lose the love and mercy of Allah?

For instance Christians do not commit any bombing or suicide attacks against other religions.

The Sunnites want to expand their Islam worldwide. Is it the will of Allah to do this with fighting against Shiites and believers of other religions? Or will Allah only be pleased by Sunnites who live a life according the will of Allah, which will be a peaceable life?

It is an indisputable right of Muslims to proselytize for the religion of Islam. That will be more successful when Muslims exemplify their belief with a peaceful, moral and ethically fascinating life.

To make peace between various religions and also inside of Islam related to different sects in Islam for example between Sunnis and Shiites, Sunnis and Alawites etc. all these sects should be accepted as of equal value. They all profess to believe in God and they worship God. If tolerance is part of Islam why is tolerance not applied in relation to other religions or sects?

The governments of Islamic states are requested not to persecute further or to hinder believers of Islamic sects or other religions. It is known, that the Turkey state persecutes Alevites and obstructs Christians. Iran persecutes the followers of the Bahai religion.

The Roman Catholic Church tried in a thirty years lasting war on German territory, from 1618 until 1648, to eliminate the secession of followers of Christian Protestant belief. They had absolutely no success. Nowadays live members of Roman Catholic Church and members of Protestant denominations peacefully together in the whole world.

The conclusion is that with a war or single combats representatives of one religion cannot eliminate any other religion. The belief of a religion takes its strength from God. This strength takes effect from a higher level onto the material sphere. Wars and single fights don't get power from God. In wars and combats are only the physical forces of men effective and the force of the devil.

People can kill other people and burden their soul with a sin. But they cannot kill any belief in God based on a religion, which is widely spread in the world.

It should be the task of the convention to lay down in the revised Koran for Islam 3.0 the principles to keep peace with other human beings and especially the believers of other religions. This should include the principles for respecting the believers of other sects and religions. The convention has to make it generally binding for all Muslims.

All Muslims in a world of peace have to be taught to respect the believers of Islamic sects and other religions as coequal.

If the Sunnis are really more religious than Shiites they should enjoy the advantages affiliated with this. If Sunnis practice a deep spirituality instead of only executing schematically the prescribed rituals they have a closer contact with Allah. This makes them happy. They receive more energy and a better concentration from Allah to execute their daily tasks. They will become more successful than less religious people.

Abdel-Hakim Ourghy, leader of the department for Islamic Theology and Religious Education at the Pädagogische Hochschule (College of Education) Freiburg, Germany, wrote an article about "Religion und Gewalt – Der Islam braucht eine kritikfähige Renaissance" (English: Religion and Violence – Islam needs a Renaissance in which Criticism is accepted), published in Süddeutsche Zeitung, 20.01.2015: in his article he has warned: "An insistence on the absolute and universal truth claim of Islam ever means intolerance and dehumanization of other religions".

If I don't be wrong the Islam raises the pretense to be a religion of peace and justice. How is it in all Islamic states in the world? Live all people in these Islamic states in peace and in justice? If this is not the case wouldn't it be more reasonable to hang this pretense a bit lower?

Freedom to Join or to Leave Islam

There is the question of freedom to join the Islam but being not allowed to leave the Islam. Some Islamic states convict people to death who leave the Islam or want to leave this religion. This is bondage. It is incompatible with the God-given freedom.

This bondage should be reviewed if it is compatible with the freedom of people given by God. God wants that his human beings voluntarily love and worship him not because they were forced to do this.

The Christian Protestant Churches and the Roman Catholic Church give all people the freedom to become a member of their church and anytime to give up the fellowship. Both organizations have opened themselves more and more to the so-called modern world and with that losing more and more their spirituality. As a result of this "modernization" an increasing number of members leave these two organizations. But these Christian denominations would not have any advantage to oblige their members to remain in their organization. The bondage would push off people who want to worship God in a community.

Capitalism has caused a partial loss of moral and ethical standards in the western societies as well as in the Protestant denominations.

I can understand that the Islam doesn't want people in their community who can come and leave whenever they want. A possible solution to grant freedom for being a member of the Islam community, for being a Muslim or leaving the Islam, should be defined. First of all Muslims should be free to leave the Islam. But if they want to come back to the Islam community they should have to overcome some barriers to find out whether they have recognized that the Islam is their final spiritual home.

The two Faces of Islam

The above headline might confuse the readers. But it indicates that the Islam is confronted with different situations in the world and different government regulations.

Islamic States

First of all there are the Islamic states in which the Islam is state religion. In these states the law of the shari'ah as Islamic law can be valid. There are other states in which the majority of inhabitants profess to Islam.

In all these countries the devout followers of Islam can live rigid rules of the Koran. In these states Muslims must not keep up with life in modern civilizations, must not agree to equal rights of men and women. But they can decide to go the way for gender equalization.

It is recommended to determine in the revised Koran for Islam 3.0 that for girls respectively young women the minimum age for a marriage should be 16 years. The Koran should also give girls the right to visit a school.

In Cairo, Egypt, groups of young men raped young women who had gathered in groups at a public place to chat with one another. The reason for this was that the young men were convinced that it is Muslim women not allowed to leave their home and to stay at public places. It should be defined if the Koran allows young men to rape women gathering at public places because they are convinced that the women act against the Koran. Or if with their rape they burden their soul with strong sin.

It should be defined if young Muslim women have the right to meet with other women at public places just to chat with each other.

The convention should clear if the Islam stands for the destruction of ancient objects of cultural value because they show figures or images of ancient gods of pagans.

As a reminder I want to point out that Muslims with suicide attacks have only achieved that worldwide the Islam is perceived as religion of violence. It was pushed in the background that the Islam will be a religion of peace. Wouldn't it make sense to define in the Koran that suicide attacks are a sin before Allah?

Muslims could be requested to pray for justice if they feel treated unjust instead of using violence. If they have complete trust in Allah, the Almighty, and if they are free from sins their prayers will have the desired result.

Secular States

Muslims want to live in the western world but not like the western world. This plan mostly cannot be achieved.

Many states, especially the western countries, have a strict constitutional separation of church and state. That does mean also the separation of state and religion.

Muslims living in these secular states come into conflict with the law if they want to live a rigid or fundamental Islam.

The constitution of these states demands the strict observation of equal rights of men and women. Forbidden are also bigamy and polygamy.

According to the actual Koran the husband can request his wife to cohabitation with him whenever he wants. His wife has to be obedient to him.

In secular states with equal rights of men and women the wife can deny to have sexual intercourse wanted by her husband if she has no desire for this. If her husband enforces the coitus from her it is a rape. If his wife takes this rape to court her husband will be punished by a term of imprisonment of at least two years, in Germany.

I am not quite sure but it could be that in secular states it is for a woman easier to get divorced than according the Islamic law.

The gender equality gives particularly women the right and the freedom to exercise control over their own bodies and to decide when they wish to start a family. A forced marriage is forbidden and will be punished.

Women have the right to determine whether and when they leave their home and whether they take on a job or chuck a job.

In Germany law forbids it that parents beat their children.

In most of all secular states the visit of a school is obligatory. Pupils can be picked up by police and be brought to school. Parents can be convicted to pay a penalty if they refuse to send their children to school.

Honor killings by adults are punished by a term of imprisonment of at least 15 years in Germany, in other countries potentially for lifetime.

Homosexuality in western countries is protected and promoted. Homosexual men can marry one another, as well as gay women. A minority of Christians dislikes the right of homosexual people to marry one another but they are obliged to accept it.

The constitution in western countries grants religious freedom, freedom of opinion, freedom of speech and freedom of press. In practical life it has had as a result cartoons in satire magazines about the prophet Muhammad. This has led to turmoils in the Islamic world. The press, politicians and representatives of the western governments insist on the freedom of press to libel people or founders of a religion. From Muslims in western countries is demanded to endure cartoons of their prophet even if Muslims regard the cartoons as an offense of their prophet.

Muslim communities that want to maintain high moral und ethical standards are at risk that their children give up their originally learned moral and ethical behavior. This could occur as a result of the contact in school and on the job where they are confronted with permissive sexuality, alcoholism and drug consumption, maybe also with mobbing and other means of violation.

Muslims have the same rights as their fellow citizens of other religions or as the atheists. Muslims should not demand special rulings for them, which are not granted Christians in Islamic states. Otherwise they could diminish their acceptance.

The problem of Muslims in western countries is that their Koran is regarded as a possible source of terrorism. That means Islamist actions could occur against Shiites, Yazidis and Christians and other religions. The fellow citizens of Muslims regard the Islamic communities with mistrust because they fear that in these communities terrorism could grow.

It could be considered by the convention to include a recommendation in the revised Koran for Islam 3.0 that Muslims in secular states who want to practice a rather rigid Islam should leave their secular country in order not to get in conflict with the laws of their actual country.

Several years ago the grand mufti of Cairo has stated that wearing a headscarf is not obligatory for a Muslim woman but that it is only a matter of tradition. It could be helpful to define if wearing a headscarf is obligatory for a Muslim woman or can be worn voluntarily.

Many non-Muslim inhabitants rather regard women with a headscarf as foreigners. It is also a disadvantage of women with headscarf to find a job because of their bothersome appearance. The headscarf of a Muslim woman is perceived as an annoying symbol and as a symbol for the suppression of women but also as a symbol for her Islamic belief. In enterprises in secular states it is absolutely unusual that employees wear a symbol of their religion. It is unwanted that employees witness their religion with a large prominent symbol.

Muslims living in secular countries want that the Islam be accepted as associated with the country and not as a foreign part. But this is not to achieve when the imams preach in mosques in a foreign language, not in the language of the country.

The convention should consider integrating into the revised Koran for Islam 3.0 a special section for Muslims living in secular states.

Loss of Importance of Religion in Western Countries

Christian religion in western countries is increasingly eroded. People have more and more less interest in spirituality and in religion. Their God is replaced on the one hand by Soccer, on the other hand by the „dance around the Golden Calf". Instead of worshipping God young people like the fun society. Although people do not behave as a Christian they believe to be a Christian.

Governments, politicians and their controlled media support this development to regard religion rather as a mythology or even as superstition. It makes it easier to influence people. With religious people it is difficult to manipulate them because they ask their God for advice and ask him to guide them.

The capitalism as economical model displaces religions with their social pretension. Thus religions have become insignificant. Religious and spiritual people are bad consumers because their life is based on higher values instead on pure consumption.

Also the Islam could be eroded by means of capitalism.

Epilogue

Societies in the western world are irritated about the Islam. They have questions that are not answered.

Many people in the world ask themselves if the Islam is a peaceful religion or a violent religion. They look at the many attacks with bombs and gunfire of Sunnis against Shiites and vice versa in Pakistan, Afghanistan, Iraq, Syria, Libya, Nigeria, Somalia, Kenya, Yemen and other countries. In many Islamic countries similar aggressions of Sunnis against Christians occur.

If there are militant actions against people, Muslims or infidels, the Muslims say that these have come from Islamists. They allege that Islamists have nothing to do with Islam and that they are terrorists.

But how can one understand this assertion?

Like the ordinary Muslim the so-called Islamists, of Sunni belief, profess their faith, pray five times a day, practice almsgiving, visit the mosque and hold the Ramadan. They may even go on pilgrimage to Mecca. What is the difference between an ordinary Sunni Muslim and an Islamist?

The Muslim endeavors to live a life according to the rules of the Koran. But also the Islamist is convinced to live according to the rules of the Koran. When Islamists are killing Christians, Yazidis and Shiites they argue that the Koran entitles them to do this. With their killing of nonbelievers they fulfill the will of Allah. Allah will reward them they believe.

Islamic religious legal scholars, imams or muftis or ayatollahs, did regularly not refute the arguments of the Islamists.

The question is, why don't they rebut the arguments of the Islamists. Could it be that really there are references in the Koran that allow the killing of infidels, also Shiites as infidels?

Another question is the role of Allah, the definition of Allah. Which values does Allah represent? Does he stand for the good, in people and in nature or also for the evil? Is Allah the god of mercy and love or also a god of rage?

In the Christian religion God is exclusively a God of love and mercy not of any rage. God has given his human beings the free will. They can decide to keep the 10 commandments and to love their neighbor as themselves or to act against God's commandments and other divine laws and in doing so to fall into sin. They have to bear the consequences of their sins, at the latest at the Last Judgment.

In Christian teaching there is God, representing the good, and his adversary Satan, the devil, representing the evil. Christians committing sins are serving Satan, the devil.

What about Allah? Has he given his Muslims the free will? Which role does the devil play in Islamic religion?

What demands Allah of his believers, how have they to treat Non-Islamic people? If Islamists kill Non-Islamic people or even Shiites, do they serve Allah or the devil? Is there a general teaching in Islam that defines when a Muslim serves Allah or the devil? At their pilgrimage to Mecca even Islamists throw stones on the symbol of the devil. Because they do not believe to serve the devil when they kill followers of other religions. Why do not Islamic religious authorities tell the Islamists that they serve the devil when committing terroristic attacks and killings?

It was proven that the Palestinians couldn't free themselves from the occupation by Israel by application of violence. But there is a better possibility to reach this target.

I recommend that Muslims worldwide pray for justice and for freedom for their Palestinian brothers and sisters that suffer under the occupying power of Israel. How to achieve with prayers the wanted results I have described this in my book-trilogy in German language "Das FBI gegen die Macht des Gebets" published by Amazon. The book describes the power of prayer. The prayer is effective only if the target is justified before God.

Unethical Muhammad Satire of Charlie Hebdo

The Pious Muslim and Jesus Christ

A fictional story of George Curtisius

Jesus Christ has come back on earth in a human garment for a short time. He was in France, in Paris, walking unrecognized on the Montmartre. He looked at the designers making portraits of passers-by.

A very pious Muslim came along. He recognized Jesus Christ by his divine radiation. He came up to him and spoke to him. „Hi, Jesus Christ, I am a Muslim and I ask you to answer me a question." Jesus looked surprised but friendly. "What do you want to know?" he responded.

„As a Muslim I am disappointed and angrily that the cartoonists of a satire magazine disparage our Prophet Muhammad. They draw pictures of him, which is forbidden in our religion, and they mock at him and expose him to ridiculousness. Is that behavior part of the Christian religion?"

Jesus Christ looked seriously now. "You should consider two factors," he answered.

"Your society has decided to be a secular one, which is primarily a Non-Christian society. In your French society you insist on values like freedom, equality and brotherliness.

God has given all his children the free will. They can behave in a good manner or in an evil manner. But they have to bear the consequences of their decision and their subsequent behavior.

Freedom is linked with responsibility. There is no freedom without it. Freedom to act with respect to another human being means also to bear the responsibility for that what it means for the other. Freedom is called a value of the western world. A Value is something precious for everyone.

There are freedom of belief and freedom of speech and freedom of the press.

If freedom of press is used to disparage or disdain the religious feelings of another person or of many persons, this is no longer a value. It is the contradiction of a value. This type of freedom is a non-value. It is not precious at all.

The voluntary disrespect of religious feelings and their deliberate provocation is a violation of equality and of brotherliness. Disdaining the religious feelings of Muslims by disparaging their holy Prophet Muhammad is trampling on the feelings of people who adore him. Such behavior is a characteristic symptom of a lack of morality and ethics.

Freedom does not offend and does not make fun of what is other people holy. This violation of freedom is also the contradiction of tolerance! Terrorism of a minority of Muslims doesn't justify any disparagement of the religious feelings of peaceful Muslims however.

Jesus Christ made pause. Then he continued. "The second factor as to your question is the Christian teaching. To be a Christ means to be for the neighbor not against him. It means to be benevolently and sympathetically to your neighbor and having understanding for him.

As it is said in the Fourth Commandment to honor your father and your mother it should also understood that you respect your neighbor wishing him the best. Part of Christian teaching is also 'love your neighbor as yourself'. It is also said 'treat people the same way you want them to treat you'.

If caricaturists of a satire magazine purposely offend the holy feelings of their fellow citizens they appeal to the low instincts of their readers. They use their intolerable attack on Muslims only to make more profit. They abuse human rights. But this doesn't entitle belligerent Muslims to kill those persons, which blasphemed their religious feelings. They should leave it to God to ensure justice.

The behavior of caricaturists insulting the Prophet Muhammad with the result of disdaining the religious feelings of Muslims is also an infringement of Christian teachings.

I have answered your question. Pray with your brothers and sisters to God and surrender him your sorrows and pain. Trust in God that he will ensure justice at the right time."

The very pious Muslim thanked Jesus Christ for answering his question and went off.

Books of George Curtisius

In 2013 George Curtisius published his book trilogy:

"Das FBI gegen die Macht des Gebets",

as a Print version at Amazon as well as Kindle edition, digital also with epub dealers.

The book trilogy is a Christian thriller. People can get happier and more successful with the power of the prayer and the power of the forgiveness. The book contains criticism of the politics and the society of the USA, criticism of capitalism. But also something in this book is a bit satire.

December 2014, George Curtisius published his brochure at Book on Demand:

"Diktatur des Kapitalismus - Vision eines modernen Sozialismus".

The brochure can be bought at all booksellers also at Amazon.

The little book with 92 sides consists of three parts. The dictatorship of the capitalism is described first and how it has an effect on people. Our form of government is a pseudo-democracy. Morals and customs are dilapidated. Part 2 describes the failure of the German Democratic Republic (DDR) with its socialism and the reasons for it.

Part 3 develops the vision of a socialism going out of old ideas into a modern socialism with freedom, peace, justice and far-reaching equality of the living conditions for all citizens, job guarantee and social and personal safety. All citizens live in a modest prosperity. There isn't any poverty.

December 2014 George Curtisius published at Book on Demand his book:

„Friedenslösung für Ukraine, Irak/Syrien! – Konflikt-Gefahren durch Wirtschaftsflüchtlinge und Islam?" – 60 pages.

February 2015 George Curtisius published at Amazon in English language:

"Peace Solution for Ukraine and Iraq/Syria" – 38 pages.

www.ingramcontent.com/pod-product-compliance
Lightning Source LLC
Chambersburg PA
CBHW070513290526
45790CB00003B/1215